1-WEEK

MARKETING PLAN

GO FROM $1,000 TO $10,000 A WEEK

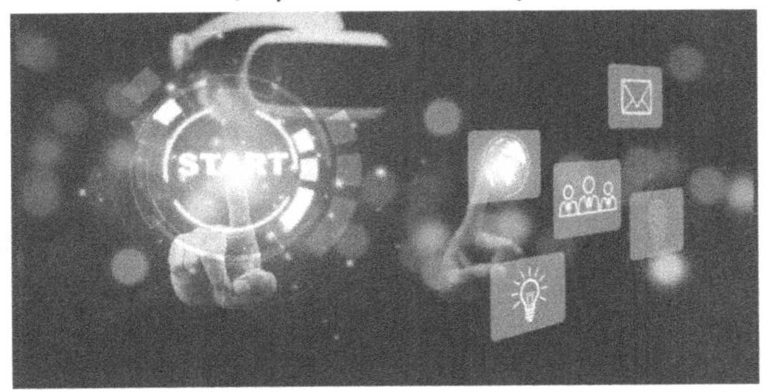

MASTER THE ACT OF STORYTELLING, MAKE IRRESISTIBLE OFFER AND IMPLEMENT THE EXPERTS SECRETS

ROBERT DONALD

Copyright © 2024 by Robert Donald

CONTENTS

ACKNOWLEDGEMENT

I wish I could tell you that every single idea in this book is my original creations and that I am a marketing and business genius.

I'd want to express my heartfelt gratitude to my colleague who helped make this endeavor possible. His continuous assistance, advice, and encouragement have been crucial throughout this journey.

Williams James: My Backbone

Williams, you have been the solid pillar upon whom I have relied during the most difficult times of this quest. Your wisdom, kindness, and unshakable confidence in my talents have driven my determination while keeping me grounded. Your help has been nothing short of extraordinary, and I will be eternally grateful for your presence in my life.

Jones Walker, more of a Brother

Jones, your friendship and camaraderie have given me courage and motivation every step of the way. Your undying loyalty, endless enthusiasm, and real companionship have greatly enhanced my life. You have always been by my side, providing unfailing support and encouragement. I am grateful for your relationship and consider you both a friend and a brother.

Therefore, your contributions have had an indelible impact on this project and molded its result in ways that cannot be measured. Your unflinching faith in me has served as a constant source of inspiration, and I consider myself extremely fortunate to have you both on my side.

INTRODUCTION

I describe my journey of self-realization and personal development in this guide, along with the actions I did to fulfill my potential and succeed. I offer a road plan for anyone looking to start their own journey of personal and professional improvement, from appreciating every accomplishment to accepting the power of learning.

If I had to summarize the importance of this book in one sentence, it would be "Money Machine." I have painstakingly put this as early as possible in the book because I wouldn't want to waste your time.

In the words of Proverbs 22:7, "The rich rule over the poor, and the borrower is slave to the lender." Touch your heart and say to yourself, I will forever remain Wealthy.

Accept Your Journey

Each journey starts with one step. It was, for me, realizing how much more capable I was than I had previously thought. I had the capacity to transform my life, impact society, and accomplish greater achievement than I could have ever imagined. However, recognizing this possibility was insufficient. I needed to do something.

I can still clearly recall the day I made the decision to walk on. It was just another day, but something inside of me had changed. I was fed up with feeling trapped and felt I was capable of so much more but didn't know how to reach my full potential. I had to change, I understood that.

I therefore began to welcome my travels. I started to view every obstacle as a chance for development, every failure as a teaching moment, and every accomplishment as proof of my potential. I turned my attention away from comparing my journey to that of others and toward my own. I came to understand that every step I took toward reaching my potential was a stride toward success— rather than a destination.

Use Knowledge to Your Advantage

Learning was the first thing I did on my adventure. I learned from successful people by soaking up their knowledge and implementing their tactics in my own life. I found that everyone could follow the route to success if they were prepared to study and develop; it wasn't a secret kept for a chosen few.

I listened to podcasts, went to seminars, and read books. I looked for mentors and took notes on their experiences. I turned into a sponge and absorbed whatever I could. And the more I discovered my ignorance, the more of it dawned on me.

But learning involved more than merely picking up facts. It involved questioning my assumptions, shifting my perspective, and becoming receptive to fresh ideas. It was all about understanding how to perceive the world not as it is, but as it may be. Above all, it was about developing self-belief and potential awareness.

Make A Change By Acting Now

Only half the fight was won by learning. Putting that information into practice was the actual problem. I had to make adjustments in my life, venture outside of my comfort zone, and take chances. Despite the difficulties, each step I took got me closer to my objectives.

I began modestly, establishing daily objectives and worked toward them. I discovered how to welcome failure—not as a setback, but as a teaching moment. I forced myself to venture outside of my comfort zone and attempt new things.

And I got bigger with each stride. I developed greater self-assurance, fortitude, and resolve. I discovered that taking action was all that stood between me and my objectives. Therefore, I did something.

Celebrate Your Success

Any accomplishment, regardless of size, deserves to be shonored. Celebrating achievement is about realizing your hard work and utilizing it as motivation to keep going forward, not about boasting or being conceited. Recall that success is a process rather than an end point. Enjoy each stage of the journey.

No matter how tiny, I've learnt to enjoy my accomplishments. All of my accomplishments, both big and small, were a result of my diligence and hard work. I discovered that being proud of my accomplishments does not imply conceit; rather, it is an acknowledgment of my hard work and dedication.

Recognizing your accomplishments is only one aspect of celebrating success, though. The key is to use their accomplishments as motivation to advance. Realizing that each accomplishment, no matter how minor, is a step toward your ultimate objective is key.

Keep Growing And Keep Believing

The path to success is a never-ending one. There will constantly be fresh obstacles to overcome, new insights to gain, and new heights to scale. But every step I take makes me stronger, more self-assured, and more competent. I have faith in my capacity to reach my goals and in my potential. You can, too.

I discovered that growth is an ongoing endeavor. It continues even after you accomplish a milestone or reach a goal. Learning, developing, and evolving is a lifelong endeavor. And every step forward makes me a better version of myself.

However, growth encompasses more than just personal growth. It all comes down to having faith in your potential and your capacity for greatness. It's about pushing yourself beyond your comfort zone to take on new tasks, achieve new heights, and continuously advance.

Continue to expand, then. Continue to learn. Persist in challenging oneself. Above all, remember to always believe in your own abilities because you have the capacity to accomplish big things. And the road to success is just getting started for you.

PART A: BRING OUT THE BEST IN YOUR BUSINESS

Section 1: Powerful Ways To Grow Quickly For Success

People who want to start their own small business are driven by a desire to make the world a better place with their product or service and the hope that they will be rewarded for their efforts until the business they started becomes a huge money-making empire.

Success stories of this kind of business can be found all over the world, from Amazon to Google to Tesla to Tata to Alibaba and many more. The list does seem to go on forever. You must want to be on this list, right?

That's the dream part. Additionally, we are aware that many small businesses around the world are having a hard time, and a good number of them close down.

Not many small businesses make more than $1 million a year. In fact, 16% of small business owners are not very successful and make less than $10,000 a year. That's reality.

Taking scales into account

For the small percentage that is profitable enough to succeed and grow because of a positive cash flow, perhaps a few can make it to become large companies, while the majority will survive as small businesses only.

If you then are one of those businesses that survive and are now on the brink of further growth, should you then scale up your business and let it grow to become a big corporation?

That decision depends on several factors. If you are taking advantage of your growing business to further expand bigger and faster by scaling, and you have resources that can be made available to you as well as a capacity to accept risk, then scaling is a viable consideration.

Risks of scaling

Scaling a business can help your business improve its capacity and reach, leading to growth in revenue and market share. In the process, you will streamline your processes, automate jobs, and reduce costs, which will lead to greater efficiency and profitability.

Oftentimes scaling needs the injection of capital typically loans from financial institutions, an external investor, or a merger (including acquisition) by another business.

Organic growth, on the other hand, is growing a business gradually over time by reinvesting gains back into the business. This will involve expanding your customer base, raising sales, and improving your products/services. Organic growth allows business owners to keep control of their company, whereas an external investor or merger would dilute that control.

However, the constant change of business climates the disruption by new technologies and greater competition are challenges you still have to face should you choose organic growth to build your business.

To change is a necessity. Failure to change could easily mean that your business will slide into its twilight years.

Scaling therefore is risky, but the upside of scaling is that you can grow very quickly in size and scope as well as profit. It, therefore is a business decision that will rest on your objectives, resources, and risk tolerance. For scaling to be successful, you will need a large investment of time, money, and resources for planning and execution.

Because scaling needs the business to take on debt or external investment, scaling must of necessity focus on efficiency, productivity, and cost-cutting. This will mean an emphasis on keeping the business lean and agile, which improves profitability.

On the other hand, spontaneous growth is more sustainable and less risky. The rise is slower and gradual, though. The goal is on increasing the customer base by improving products and services. Costs would be higher (you lose economy of scale, for example) but there is no added debt.

Section 2: Getting Your Business Ready For Scaling

Before you start on your journey to scaling though, it is important to review various aspects of your business to assess their readiness for scaling. Shortcomings identified in the review will help you to address them as you position your business to scale up.

Finance is an important factor as cash flow is the heart of a business. Pay special review to how much cash is available particularly if your company is currently paying off certain debts.

At some point, a financial assessment of the business's financial health should be finished. Various financial ratios will give you a good idea of where the financial weaknesses are for you to fix.

Listed below are some parts of your business that you must review as you prepare your business for scaling.

1. Market Research And Marketing Plan

Once the choice to scale your business is made, determine whether there is a market out there to sustain your scaling efforts.

+ The existing market that you are serving, is it big enough to sustain your enlarged business?

+ The presence of competitors is encouraging as it suggests that the market can sustain everybody, but is there room for growth still?

You can determine the market size by extrapolating from your customers and estimating the size of that target group from actual statistics that are publicly available. You can also engage your existing customers, by evaluating what factors influence them to be your customers, and then estimate how extensive these factors are in the community at large. This will help you to refine the definition of who your target audience is so that you may grasp growth opportunities that may be present.

Your research may also help to find related audience traits that your product/services can satisfy. Alternatively, based on your resources and skills you may be able to produce related products/services that can serve an entirely different market. These are choices that you can explore as you scale.

You can optimize your marketing strategy by refining your business branding and then aligning that with the qualities of your target audience. With an existing customer base, you can test out your branding and your value proposition by using design thinking methods. This will help you to improve your product/service so that you stand out from the competition.

Be mindful of changing customer trends and fads so as to respond to them effectively. With a large enough potential market of customers, go boldly to plan a marketing campaign to target your intended audience. I have in a related article; explain how you can increase the marketing ROI using similar concepts.

2. Operational Readiness

Your business group has to be prepared to scale. As your business grows rapidly in a short space of time, your business structure has to be organized into systems so that growth can be achieved coherently. Further, if you are giving a service or information products, you need to document all the steps that go into your workflow as you serve customers.

These steps, operationalized as Standard Operating Procedures (SOPs) do provide you a training manual to copy more operators. If you are digitalizing, SOPs provide a base for process improvement. Hence SOPs allow you to monitor the efficiency and effectiveness of your business processes and serve as a benchmark for the adoption of technologies for process improvement (such as Lean Six Sigma or Business Process Automation).

3. Supply Chain

A supply chain is the sum total of all the capabilities and resources that are needed to make the products those consumers want. For a service professional e.g., such as therapy providers, consumable resources may not be an important part of the supply chain, but marketing, appointment system, payment system, consultation rooms, and service support may all be important supply chain resources and capabilities that a service business needs.

Ensure that your supply chain is stable and that it can be elastic enough to cope with variable demands. That is to say that whatever the resources needed for your business must be always available and in adequate amounts for your business to move smoothly.

4. Human Resource

You can scale up the business without scaling up your human resource. This can happen if you change the business strategy such as by digitalization and automation. In a service field, if you serve the customer 1 to 1, you can scale by changing your business model to 1 to many. Whether you build up your human resource or not, this is clearly an organizational change, and change management principles must be applied here.

Therefore you have to continually engage your people to make sure they are on the same page. Proper communication can allay a lot of anxiety and fears connected with change. A constant dialogue will help your people understand what this change is about, and their part in it, and your leadership will enable them to trust you to care for them.

5. Optimize Your Organization Setup

You most probably would need to redesign your organizational structure for any scaling project. Whether you scale with digitalization and automation or change the business model, structure must support and facilitate the purpose of your business, which is to give value to customers. This is particularly important in service businesses.

For service industries, it is important that the company design, like its operations, must be customer oriented. It must emphasize innovation, teamwork, collaboration, and accountability. Using sound organization design principles build your business structure in systemic ways that allow your operations to be smooth and efficient and poise for further growth.

6. The Leadership Group

All of these things must be done, and your leadership team must be ready for the task of growing the business. Check to see if leaders at different levels have the knowledge and skills to run a larger group. Figure out if you need to hire new people or train someone in-house to take on a leading role. The leaders must be able to create an environment where people are willing to try new things, work together, and keep learning. Their ability to coach and motivate workers to do their best must be high enough that they can motivate every worker. Could it be that the leadership team also needs coaching to bring out the best in them?

7. Controlling money

If you've looked at your company's finances, you should have a good idea of how strong they are. These will help you make your cash plans when you scale.

Make sure to spot any potential risks and areas that need improvement. Be sure the financial systems that your accountant set up are capable of accurate accounting, reporting, and planning processes. Regular monitoring and analysis of financial performance help you make informed choices whenever you need them.

Since you are scaling up, secure in-advance funding options from different financial institutions. This can be in the form of pre-approved loans, lines of credit, grants, or external partners to secure the funds when you need them. Work with your accountant to find the best financing approach.

After going through the 7 planning steps you need to take to prepare your small business to scale, you may be feeling somewhat intimidated. That is perhaps not surprising.

When you look at the upside of growth, here's why businesses want to scale. It will bring your small business to a whole new level. Whether your goal is to do a public listing, rule your niche, or go global, this is the way up. But there are risks—quite serious risks—and you can end up in failure. Hence the need to prepare and make sure your business is strong enough to handle the risks.

Have guts, fortify your company and yourself, take a bite out of the deal, and flee. Put up a lot of effort and work safely. Unless you are overcome by a black swan occurrence, you will usually survive.

CONTENT
IS KING

Marketing Strategy
1 000 000$

PART B: THE 5 KEYS TO MARKETING SUCCESS

A Successful Marketing Strategy Must Include Five Key Elements/Sections

Section 1: A Clear Understanding Of The Target Audience

Who are Your Target Audience?

The particular consumer group most likely to be interested in your product or service—and hence, the target audience for your advertising campaigns—is referred to as your target audience. Age, gender, income, region, interests, and a host of other variables may determine the target audience.

Your target market may be more general or more specialized, depending on what you sell. If you were a shoe merchant, for instance, you would have a wide target market because everyone wears shoes—men, women, and children. However, it's possible that you only provide high-tech running shoes. Then, elite athletes in the 20–40 age range who have either indicated interest in running or completed a marathon would be your target market. In any case, you need identify and categorize your target market to find the channels they favor and the creative messaging that will appeal to them.

Target Audience Examples

A certain set of people is the focus of target audiences. Men, women, teens, and kids can all be among them. Most of the time, they have a similar interest, like soccer, running, or reading. Advertisers can use personas to look up suitable trade journals or magazine titles.

The Advantages of Understanding Your Target Market

Knowing your target market is essential if you're a marketer. All of your marketing strategies and plans will be defined by this information. Although running an advertisement during the Super Bowl could seem like a terrific approach to reach as many people as possible, the cost of doing so is equally high. Not to mention that only 25% of the audience would genuinely be interested in your offering. Your advertisement will be seen by fewer people, but by the correct ones, if you know that your target demographic watches or reads a particular show or newspaper.

For instance, your target group would be better served by advertisements in running periodicals if you offer running shoes. Achieving a marketing return on investment requires careful media selection.

Knowing your target market helps you not only boost return on investment (ROI) but also improve customer relations and connection building. You may create content that appeals to particular personas and create brands that reflect the beliefs and interests of the people who are most likely to buy the product. In an era where customers demand highly targeted and personalized advertisements, this is extremely crucial. As a matter of fact, eighty percent of customers assert that they are inclined to conduct business with a company that provides personalized interactions.

Which Kinds of Audiences Are the Targets?

Target audiences can be further divided into groups based on references, intents, locations, interests, and other factors. Here are some illustrations of how you might segment your target market:

Interested

Sort the groups according to their varied interests, such as pastimes and preferred forms of entertainment. By doing this, you can create highly tailored, data-driven content that connects with your audience and encourages brand loyalty.

Purchase Intention

Define consumer groups that have a certain product in mind, such a new car or entertainment system. By doing this, you'll be better able to identify the issues that your audience is facing and develop messages that specifically meet their needs.

Subgroups

Groups of people with similar experiences, such music genres or fandoms in the entertainment industry, are referred to as subcultures. You can better comprehend who you're attempting to connect with if you know a little bit about the motives of your target audience.

What Separates a Target Market from a Target Audience?

A company's target market is the group of customers it intends to sell to or reach through marketing initiatives.

The group or section of that target market that is receiving advertisements is known as the target audience. As a result, the target market's target audience becomes a more narrowly defined subset.

Returning to the running shoe scenario, let's imagine you are running a marathon and want to offer marathon runners a deal at your Boston location. Not all marathon runners, but potential Boston Marathon participants would be the intended demographic for an advertisement promoting the deal.

Given that it is a particular subset of the broader market group, target audience and target market are frequently used synonymously. Target audience isn't usually synonymous with target market, though.

Recognizing the Functions of Your Target Market

Knowing your target audience's position in the route to buy is just as important as researching their demographics. This is an essential first step in understanding your target audience. These role frequently fall into one of the following categories:

The Decision Maker: This individual is in charge of deciding what to buy in the end. The decision-maker and the backer may or may not be the same person in some situations. When things differ, you have to accept it and adjust your advertising to the decision-maker. For instance, consider the 2010 makeover of the Old Spice brand. The company intended to update its offering in order to appeal to a younger market. After learning that women were the ones making the purchases even though males might eventually use their goods, the creative team decided to concentrate on this target market.

The Adhérent: The backer will have a significant impact on whether or not an item is purchased, even if they may not have the authority to decide. For instance, a youngster might not make the purchase directly, but they can still have an impact on it if they want something for Christmas.

For this reason, creating messaging that appeal to customers in each of these capacities is crucial.

7 Methods to Ascertain Who Your Target Market Is

It will take time to identify your target audience from the data you obtain from customer interactions. You will also need to optimize as new information becomes available and assess existing purchasing patterns and buyer trends.

Realizing Your Target Audience Should Be Made Easier With The Following Steps:

1. Examine Your Clientele and Conduct Interviews with Them

Examining the people who have already purchased your goods or service is one of the finest ways to identify your target market. What are their interests, what is their age, and where do they reside? Customer surveys or social media interaction are effective ways to find out this information.

2. Carry out Industry Trend Analysis and Market Research

To find out what gaps in the market your product can fill, look at the market research conducted for your sector. Examine popular items to determine where they are concentrating their efforts, and then focus even more on the distinctive features of your own product.

3. Examine the Rivals

By observing their competitors' target audience and sales strategy, marketers can gain valuable insights. Do they employ offline or online channels? Do they have the supporter or the decision-maker in mind?

4. Develop Personas

Developing personas is an excellent method for narrowing down the distinct groups that comprise your intended audience. If your product appeals to a broad range of customers, this is quite beneficial. You can ascertain the broad characteristics, character traits, and requirements of your intended audience by using personas. Different demands will be addressed by the "Fran First-Time Runner" character than by the **"Sam Seasoned Pro."** In order to provide marketers with a more comprehensive understanding of the buyer, personas are developed using data, surveys, digital interactions, and any other information available. This could include preferred pastimes, TV series, magazines, etc. It is advised that marketers create three to five personas.

5. Define Who Is Not Your Target Audience

Undoubtedly, there will be customers who fall within your target market but ignore messages. When defining your audience, make an effort to be as exact as possible Which women make up your demographic—those in the 20–40 age range? Your teams won't waste advertising dollars on unprofitable segments if they are aware of this.

6. Always Review

You will gain an ever-more precise understanding of your target audiences as you collect more data and engage with consumers. Knowing this means that in order to get the greatest outcomes, personas need to be continuously optimized and refined.

7. Adopt Google Analytics

A wealth of information about the people who visit your website may be found using Google Analytics. Making more data-driven decisions during the media planning process is possible with the help of this information, which can be used to uncover important insights like the channels your target audience is using or the kinds of content they love and connect with the most.

Social

You may target adverts on social media according to different interests and demographics. Diverse groups consume media in different ways, despite the audience being highly exact. On Facebook, certain individuals could react better to business-related ads than they would on Instagram. The effectiveness of various ad formats on these platforms, such as display versus native, should also be measured. Try a variety of platforms to find what produces the best results.

You may find out which media channels and television programs your target viewers watch by using third-party information marketing analytics tools like the Marketing Measurement and Attribution Platform. Look at these businesses' methods for determining how to connect with their target markets before choosing a partner. Do they have media relationships or are they utilizing old data?

The Appropriate Time to Reach Your Audience

Knowing not just where to reach but also when to reach today's empowered consumers is crucial for effective marketing. Optimal timing in marketing will pay off as customers get increasingly skilled at blocking out messages.

To guarantee timely marketing through a variety of media, there are a few key factors to check:

Watch TV

DVR technology has made it unnecessary for viewers to endure advertisements. This implies that you can't always count on advertising during a show's intermission to receive views, even if you have the correct target demographic. Aim to be the final commercial to air at the conclusion of a break or the first one to air before one. Live television is even better, whether it's for sports or the late-night news. More people are definitely watching right now rather than using the quick forward button because these are live.

Radio

Booking advertisements for when the commercial break begins or ends is advisable, as listeners frequently switch radio stations during these periods. DMAs (Designated Market Areas) should also be taken into consideration. Nielsen offers DMAs, which are determined by the strength of the signal. Southern New Hampshire and Rhode Island, for instance, are part of the Boston market. Radio can be an excellent tool for reaching local consumers, but it can also attract listeners from outside your target area, so it's vital to keep that in mind.

Email

An email sent on a different day may have a higher open rate than one sent on a Friday as Fridays are typically taken off by people (unless the data indicates otherwise).

Approaching your audience using social media sites such as Instagram, Facebook, Twitter, and WhatsApp may be quite successful if done well. An overview of each platform's functionality may be found here.

WhatsApp Group:

- **Establish Groups:** on begin, establish groups according on shared interests, audience topics, or demographics.
- **Participate Actively:** Let the groups know about important changes, promotions, special deals, and useful content.

- To maintain member engagement, promote dialogues, surveys, and question-and-answer sessions.
- **Respect privacy:** Prior to adding someone to a group, be sure you have their consent and honor their choices on privacy.

Facebook

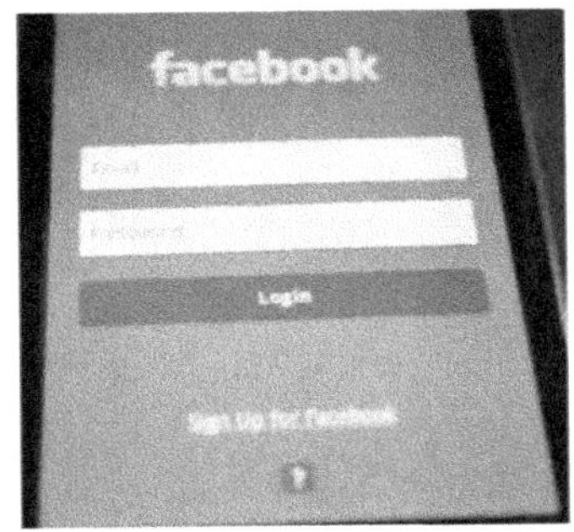

- **Make a Page or Group:** Based on your objectives, make a Group to foster community engagement or a Page for your brand or company.
- **Share a Variety of Information:** Post a range of information, including news, events, pictures, videos, surveys, and behind-the-scenes looks.

- **Engage with Fans:** To establish a connection with your followers, reply to messages, reviews, and comments right away.

- **Use Facebook Live To Your Advantage:** To interact with your audience directly, host live Q&A sessions, product demos, or interviews.

Twitter

- To stay visible in the feeds of your followers, post on Twitter often.

- **Diligently Employ Hashtags:** To improve discoverability and reach a wider audience, include pertinent hashtags.

- **Participate in Conversations:** Retweet pertinent information, discuss hot subjects with your followers, and respond to mentions.

- To achieve customized communication, use Twitter Lists to group your followers according to their interests or demographics.

Instagram

+ **Visual Storytelling:** Post excellent photos and videos that complement the tone and messaging of your company.

+ **Make Use of Stories and Reels:** Upload behind-the-scenes photos, surveys, and Q&A sessions to Instagram Stories. For short-form video content, try out Reels.

+ **Interact with Fans:** Post user-generated material (UGC) and provide credit when you reply to remarks or direct messages.

+ **Collaborate with Influencers:** To reach their following and grow your audience, collaborate with influencers in your niche.

General Tips:

Consistency: To keep your audience interested and aware of you, stick to a consistent posting schedule.

Analytics: Monitor content performance using platform analytics and modify your approach as necessary.

Cross-Promotion: To improve exposure and draw in followers from various sources, cross-promote your social media profiles on several networks.

Be Realistic: Give your audience something of value, avoid posting stuff that is unduly commercial, and be authentic in your interactions.

You may connect with and interact with your audience through the effective use of various social media platforms, which will help you create a vibrant online community that is centered around your business or message.

Section 2: A Unique Value Proposition

Unique Value Proposition is an effective way to convey the worth of your goods or services which is sometimes known as a UVP or value prop. It highlights the advantages of your product, how it meets the needs of clients, and how it stands out from competing supplies.

A customer should choose you above your competition for a reason, and that is what your unique value proposition (UVP) means;

Prior to selecting a product or service, customers usually compare several of them. UVP is what makes you stand out from the crowd.

When a visitor lands on your homepage, product page, or landing page, it has to be the first thing they will see and a key component of your advertising initiatives.

What a Mission Statement or Tagline Is, Is Not What a Unique Value Proposition Is

What you have to offer and why a customer should choose you are explained in a UVP. Customer influence is similar between mission statements and taglines.

They function differently from a value proposition, though. You can define your purpose in life with a mission statement. It explains your company's objective.

Here is an example of Nike's goal statement: "To inspire and innovate for every athlete on the planet." A catchy, brief phrase that sums up your brand's essence is called a tagline or slogan.

"Just Do It" is Nike's tagline.

Although you should use mission statements and taglines in your business marketing, your value prop should always come first.

For what reason?

The reason being that a value prop is a specific claim about your commodity or service. Nike's value proposition for their line of personalized shoes is as follows.

The process of creating your own Nike begins here. With Nike By You, you can design your own legendary sneakers and give them something they've never seen before.

Particular to the product is this UVP. In a manner that a goal statement or tagline cannot, it explains to clients why Nike By You is the ideal answer for their present need.

To put it briefly...

- Mission statement = business goal
- Tagline = brand essence or idea
- Value prop = product or service value

Comparing a Unique Selling Proposition with a Unique Value Proposition

There is a common confusion between USPs and unique value propositions (UVPs).

There is a distinction, though:

- A distinctive value proposition elucidates the reasons behind consumers' care and the benefits they receive.
- A unique selling proposition outlines what sets you apart.

Here is Robinhood's USP.

"Investing for everyone"

Regardless of your level of investment experience, Robinhood is an inclusive platform for investors. That benefit is sold by its USP.

And now for its UVP:

"Start with just \$1 to build your portfolio. Invest without paying commissions in stocks, options, and ETFs at your own speed.

The UVP enables buyers to recognize the product's real value.

You may leverage your product's unique selling point to create a value prop because it encapsulates what makes it special.

Robinhood's USP is informed, for instance, by its UVP headline, "Build your portfolio starting with just \$1." \$1 is hardly a high entry barrier. This phrase also means "investing for everyone."

Your marketing plan should emphasize both value propositions and distinctive selling points.

You may grab the attention of your audience by using USPs. Potential consumers are encouraged to take action based on UVPs.

How Do You Create a Great Unique Value Proposition?

A strong value proposition

- It tells a consumer what they'll get by purchasing your product or service;
- It is brief and easy to comprehend;
- It is memorable;
- It explains how your offer differs from the competition.

A UVP usually consists of **three primary components** in order to convey value to the reader right away:

- A catchy title that highlights the key advantage
- A subheading, paragraph, or series of bullet points outlining your offering and its benefits;
- An image, graphic, or video showcasing your product or service and reinforcing the message.

Trello's homepage demonstrates what a strong proposition looks like:

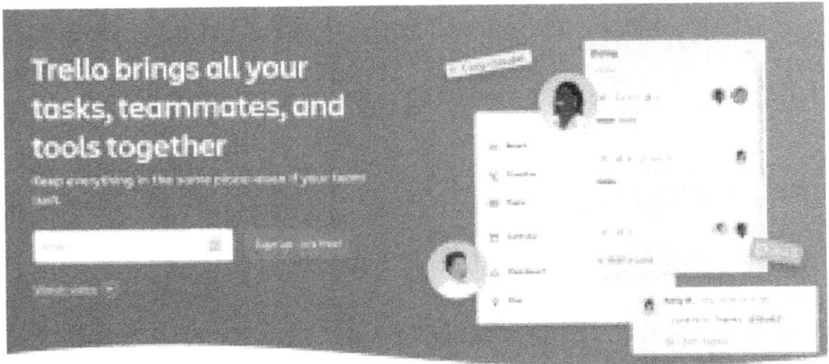

The rationale behind its effectiveness is as follows:

- The title makes it apparent what Trello does and who it is intended for
- The subheading details how Trello keeps remote teams organized
- An appropriate picture displays groups working together.

Trello uses the fact that users can manage several projects in one location to effectively pitch the benefits of their platform in just twenty words.

It eliminates the need for teams to communicate via a variety of channels and the problems that arise from doing so (such as missing deadlines, protracted assignments, and never-ending email chains).

To win over a customer, a strong UVP may also incorporate an extra selling factor. These are minor details that somewhat increase the attractiveness of an offer. Trello updates the call-to-action (CTA) in the example above to read, "Sign up – it's free." For consumers on a tight budget, "it's free" is a useful extra.

Some typical selling points are:

- Free shipping
- Delivery the next day
- No commitment
- Cancel at any moment
- Purchase now and save

A consumer may be persuaded to pick you over a rival by these factors, which can tip the odds in your favor.

Types of Unique Value Proposition

One of four themes usually encompasses unique value propositions:

1. Best-value item or service
2. The best available good or service
3. The most opulent item
4. Essential (required) item

Buyer motives are reflected in these themes. Frequently, consumers base their purchases on one or more of the following:

- **Value for money:** They're looking for the best value in terms of price and quality.
- **Reputation:** They are looking for the industry leader or a business with a solid track record.
- **Status:** They seek out goods or services that symbolize opulence.
- **Need:** The product is a need (a plumber, for example, cannot function without a pipe wrench).

A strong value proposition emphasizes these elements in order to give what clients value most.

Be certain of the services you wish to provide to clients before you begin working on your value offer.

- Do you offer goods and services at lower prices than your rivals? • Is your brand more well-known?
- Do you provide services or goods for luxury?
- Do you provide clients with goods and services that they cannot live without?

How To Formulate Your Unique Value Proposition

In order for your value proposition to be effective, you must have a thorough understanding of your target market, your offering, and how your goods or services fits into the life of the client.

Write a UVP without considering what you believe to be true. To ensure that it will draw in your intended audience, base it on testing and research.

Here's How To Create A Special Value Proposition:

Find the main pain points by conducting customer analysis

Customer analysis is the process of using data to comprehend the needs, desires, and pain points of your target audience. A UVP that speaks to your clients' needs can be created if you understand what motivates them.

Choose **five to ten** of your most devoted clients to survey or interview from your CRM (Customer Relationship Management) platform to get things started.

In the event that you do not yet have many or any customers, you can locate interview subjects by doing the following:

- Contacting members of relevant Facebook, LinkedIn, or niche forums
- Contacting social media followers or users who interact with your competitors
- Going to industry networking events

Collaborating with a market research firm Inquire about the participants' reasons for purchasing. For instance:

- What are the primary problems you are having with X?
- What were you searching for in X?
- What did you want X to assist you in achieving?
- Which would you prefer, X or Y? Why is it the case?
- What price would you set for X?

Add customer feedback to your questionnaires or interviews.

Examine:

- Positive customer feedback
- Brand mentions on social media
- Social media posts
- Requests for customer help

Understanding the issues and objectives of your audience can be gained from all of these sources.

In your investigation, look for recurring themes. You can include solutions for the recurring demands, issues, and motivations in your value proposition.

The Following Resources Will Teach You Step-By-Step How To Do Market And Customer Research:

- A Comprehensive Guide to (Successful) Customer Analysis
- How to Make the Perfect Customer Profile Template
- What Is and How to Do Market Research

Determine What Sets Your Product or Service Apart.

Your differentiators are the special qualities that make you stand out from the crowd. Customers pick you over a competitor for these reasons.

- ✓ Asking yourself what makes your product or service superior to others might help you identify your differentiators.

- ✓ Jot down the precise features of your good or service that clients find appealing.

This could include your product's usefulness, customer support, components, or cost. This task will be aided by your customer research.

For instance, Apple claims that its closed product ecosystem and design ethos set it apart from competitors.

Compared to Android smart phones, which use software from various firms, these make Apple goods feel more upscale and special

When creating your list, be careful not to add attributes that others can duplicate.

For example, "free shipping" is a pleasant and effective addition to your UVP. However, it does not distinguish you.

Once you've compiled your list, develop a competitor comparison chart to compare your capabilities to those of your competitors.

Create a Value Proposition Canvas.

A value proposition canvas looks at the aspects of your business that lead to a strong UVP.

It's intended to assist you understand the value of your product or service and how it aligns with what the customer wants.

Begin with the customer profile. You can utilize the information from your customer analysis to complete this part.

- **Gains:** What do buyers expect from you when purchasing your goods or service?
- Identify your customer's task or problem to solve with your product or service.
- **Pains:** What unfavorable experiences or risks do customers face when attempting to resolve their issues?

Now move on to the value proposition map. This outlines what your product or service provides to the customer.

- ❖ Identify customer-valued features and perks to attract creators.
- ❖ **Pain relievers:** How does your product or service help clients overcome pain?
- ❖ What items and services provide the most value to your clients and alleviate their pain?

Organize elements by marking them as "nice-to-have" or "must-have."

For example, if you own an online coffee shop, coffee subscriptions are a "must-have." Customers can use these to determine the type and quantity of coffee they require.

Branded mugs are "nice to have." They make customers pleased, but they are not necessary for the primary product.

When the value proposition map covers the most significant problems and gains in the client profile, you have a fit.

Write Your Own Value Proposition.

After determining your competitive advantage, brainstorm ideas to create a unique value proposition.

To create a simple value proposition, use the Steve Blank formula: "We help (X) do (Y) by doing (Z)."

This formula allows you to highlight benefits over features in order to appeal to your target audience's goals and needs.

A web design agency could offer a distinct value proposition such as "We help small business owners grow their audience with attractive, affordable websites."

Alternatively, you may use **Geoffrey Moore's** value positioning statement.

In his book "Crossing the Chasm," Fortune 500 firms employ a formula to establish unique value propositions by focusing on industry, category, and value: "For (target customer) who (need or potential), our (item or service brand) is (product category) that (profit)."

A value proposition for a web design studio could be "Rockstar Websites is an ecommerce platform that helps small businesses grow online without requiring technical expertise."

Steve Blank's methodology might inspire a fascinating headline, whilst Geoff Moore's method might assist you come up with key benefits for a subtitle.

However, this is a creative activity. So don't worry if you don't perfectly adhere to each template. The aim is to use them to communicate your value proposition and inspire creativity. Test Your Unique Value Proposition With a Small Audience.

The true test of a UVP is how your target audience reacts. Testing provides crucial information into what resonates and what needs to be improved in order to increase your conversion rate.

To accomplish so, you must present your value proposition statement to your target audience.

Return to the customers you interviewed to solicit feedback, or use a platform like Wynter to get your message in front of your intended audience.

Determine if the audience finds the message clear, relevant, wants the offered value, and prefers you over alternatives.

In a nutshell, strong UVP examples include:

- Apple encourages "Think Different."
- Nike: "Just do it."
- Slack message: "Be less busy."
- Amazon has been described as "Earth's most customer-centric company."
- Uber: "Get there faster."

Remember that your unique selling point (UVP) is an essential component of your brand messaging and should be integrated into all of your marketing efforts. It's what distinguishes you in a crowded market and attracts clients who share your unique value offer.

Section 3: Effective Communication Channels.

Digital Channels:

- **Email:** Send personalized messages for newsletters, promotions, updates, and customer communication.
- Use social media platforms such as Facebook, Twitter, Instagram, and LinkedIn to connect with your audience, share content, and establish communities.
- Use a website or blog to provide articles, announcements, and product information, as well as engage visitors with comments and forms.
- Mobile apps offer direct communication with users via push alerts, in-app messages, and updates.

Traditional Media:

- Print media, such as newspapers, magazines, pamphlets, and flyers, can reach local or specialty audiences.

- Broadcast advertising, interviews, or sponsored material on television and radio to increase brand visibility and reach.

- **Direct Mail:** Use physical mailings, postcards, and catalogs to target marketing initiatives.

In-Person Channels:

- **Face-to-Face Meetings:** Individual or group talks, negotiations, and relationship building.

- Conferences/Events include presentations, workshops, networking opportunities, product/service showcasing, and thought leadership.

- Networking events include casual meets, industry mixers, and professional associations to establish connections and collaborations.

Internal Communication Channels:

- **Intranet/Employee Portals:** Centralized platforms for sharing company news, policies, resources, and encouraging cooperation.
- Regular team meetings (in-person and virtual) for updates, brainstorming, and problem-solving.
- Internal Newsletters: Provide regular updates on company achievements, employee spotlights, and planned activities.

Specialized Channels:

- **Customer Support Channels:** Helpdesk, live chat, and phone support for inquiries, issues, and feedback.
- Manage public perception and media coverage through press releases, pitches, interviews, and conferences.
- Community Forums/Groups: Use online forums, discussion boards, or specialized interest groups to

connect with specialist communities and address shared concerns.

Emerging Channels:

- **Podcasts:** Audio material for narrative, interviews, and thought leadership to specific niche audiences.
- Webinars include educational information, product demos, and lead generation. They can be live or recorded.
- AI-powered chatbots provide automated customer support and conversations.

Cross-Channel Integration:

- **Omnichannel Strategy:** Integrating different communication channels for a consistent experience across all platforms.
- Optimizing communication strategies and channels using analytics and feedback loops.

Understanding your audience's preferences, the nature of the message, and your overall goals is necessary for choosing the best communication channels. To effectively reach a varied audience, a variety of methods are often required. Regular evaluation and customization in response to feedback and analytics ensures that your communication efforts are constantly improving and relevant.

Section 4 & 5: Establish A Clear Brand Identity And Develop A Strategy For Measuring And Modifying It As Appropriate.

Creating a well-defined brand identity is essential for projecting a clear and consistent picture that resonates with your target audience. Here's how to make one, followed by a strategy for evaluating its performance.

Clearly Defined Brand Identity:

❖ Define your brand's purpose and values beyond selling items or services. What ideals does your brand represent? How does it intend to impact people's lives or the world?

- ❖ **Brand Personality**:
  - o Identify the personality attributes that embody your brand. Is it fun, sophisticated, dependable, or innovative? These characteristics should be consistent throughout all communication channels.

- ❖ **Visual Identity:**
  - o Create a memorable logo, color palette, fonts, and consistent visual elements to express your brand's personality (e.g., graphics, photographic style).

- ❖ Create rules for your brand's tone, vocabulary, and messaging style. Consider how your brand interacts with its target audience: should it be formal, conversational, or authoritative?

- ❖ Define your target audience's demographics, behaviors, interests, and pain areas. Understanding your target demographic allows you to tailor your brand identity so that it resonates with then effectively.

❖ Competitive Analysis: o Analyze competitors brand identities to find gaps or chances for differentiation. Make your brand stand out in a congested marketplace.

Plan To Measure And Change The Strategy As Necessary.

Plan for Measuring and Adjusting Strategy

❖ Set Clear Goals and KPIs:

    o Create quantifiable objectives that correspond with your business goals. Define key performance indicators (KPIs) to measure progress and success.

    o Goals may include raising brand exposure, increasing website traffic, generating leads, or improving customer interaction.

❖ Track and analyze performance using;

- o Technologies like Google Analytics, social media insights, and CRM systems across several channels.
- o Evaluate the performance of your plan by tracking indicators like website traffic, conversion rates, engagement, and feedback.

❖ Conduct regular performance assessments against set KPIs.

- o Determine the strengths of the success along with progress.
- o Analyze data trends and patterns to understand audience behavior and preferences.

❖ Modify Strategy To

- o Improve your marketing plan, use performance insights to make data-driven adjustments.
- o Test different methods, channels, messaging, and targeting strategies to improve results.

- o Continuously iterate and adjust your approach depending on real-time input and changing market conditions.
- ❖ Be Agile and Flexible:
  - o Adapt swiftly to changes in customer behavior, industry trends, and competitive landscape.
  - o Maintain agility in strategy implementation, allowing for quick testing and optimization based on feedback.
- ❖ Encourage open communication and collaboration among marketing, sales, product, and other departments.
  - o Collaborate on performance insights and tactics to align and maximize effect.

MARKETING STRATEGY

PART C: MASTER THE ACT OF STORYTELLING.

Section 1: Building Your StoryBrand

Donald Miller's "Building Your StoryBrand" methodology can help create captivating marketing narratives. Let's break down the important components utilizing the character, problem, guidance, plan, call to action, failure prevention, and success:

Character:

Use the target audience or consumer as the protagonist in your story. This could refer to an individual or a group of people dealing with a certain difficulty or problem.

Problem:

Clearly state the problem or struggle your character faces. This issue should resonate with your audience and elicit a sense of urgency or concern.

Guide:

Introduce your brand or product as a guide in the story. Position yourself as the character's expert or valued advisor, able to help them conquer their obstacles.

Plan:

Provide a clear and actionable remedy for the character's predicament. This plan should show how your product or service may provide a useful and successful solution.

Call to Action:

Encourage your audience to take a specific action that coincides with your marketing objectives. This could include completing a purchase, signing up for a service, or subscribing to a newsletter.

Avoiding Failure:

Identify the risks of not taking action to address the problem. Demonstrate how your idea will assist the character avoid these bad consequences.

Success:

Show how the character will profit from implementing your plan. Create a vivid image of how their life or position will better as a result of their interaction with your business.

Example:

Character: Sarah, a busy professional who struggles to stay organized.

Problem: Sarah's workload is overwhelming, and she frequently forgets critical assignments and deadlines.

Guide: XYZ Productivity App touts itself as Sarah's reliable partner, providing tools and resources to help her manage her chores and time more successfully.

Plan: The app's customized task lists, reminders, and time-tracking capabilities will help Sarah prioritize her work and stay on track.

Call to Action: Get the app immediately and start reclaiming control over your time and productivity.

Avoiding Failure: Without an efficient productivity solution, Sarah risks missing deadlines, becoming exhausted, and falling behind in her job.

Success: Sarah feels more organized, productive, and in control of her job after using the XYZ Productivity App. She consistently fulfills deadlines and maintains better work-life balance.

Using this narrative framework in your marketing message can capture your audience's attention, resonate with their needs, and encourage them to take action, resulting in increased engagement and conversion.

Section 2: Make An Irresistible Offer

Get to Know Your Audience:

+ Learn all you can about your target audience's wants, requirements, problems, and purchasing habits by conducting extensive research.

+ Personalize your offer so it caters to a particular issue or wish that strikes a chord with your target market.

Provide Clear Value:

+ Communicate your offer's value proposition. When possible, quantify the value of the offer, such as savings, time saved, or additional features.

+ Emphasize the benefits and outcomes for customers.

Differentiate Your Offer:

- Identify what sets your offer apart from competitors'. This could include exclusive features, bonuses, assurances, or a unique selling proposition (USP).
- Highlight any additional perks or incentives that differentiate your offer.

Create a Sense of Urgency:

- Utilize scarcity and urgency strategies to instill fear of missing out (FOMO). Set a deadline or restrict the availability of the offer to encourage prompt action.
- Highlight any limited discounts, perks, or product/service availability.

Offer Risk-Free Guarantees

- This could include a money-back guarantee, a satisfaction assurance, or a free trial period.

- Reducing perceived risk leads to increased trust and conversions.

Provide Social Proof:

- Use testimonials, reviews, case studies, or endorsements to show the value and usefulness of your offer.
- Social proof increases credibility and trust among potential customers by demonstrating that others have had great experiences with your product/service.

Make Redeeming Easy:

- Make the offer redemption process simple and easy to understand. Remove any hurdles or friction that may prevent customers from taking action.
- Provide clear instructions and make the offer accessible across all marketing platforms.

Personalize the Offer:

- Segment your audience and tailor the offer to their preferences, habits, or demographics.
- Customize messaging and incentives to resonate with each category for greater relevance and effectiveness.

Test and Iterate:

- Optimize your offer's performance by continuously testing pricing, bonuses, and messaging.
- Analyze data and feedback to identify what resonates with your audience and make any improvements.

Promote Effectively:

- Use many channels to promote your compelling offer, such as email marketing, social media, paid advertising, and website promotion. • Customize your messaging and creative materials for each channel and audience segment to maximize effect.

By adopting these tactics, you can develop an appealing offer that attracts your audience's attention, generates engagement, and, eventually, increases conversions and purchases.

Section 3: Pricing, an Effective Tool

Pricing is a vital component of marketing strategy that has a substantial impact on a company's success. Here's why pricing is an important instrument in marketing.

- ❖ **Perceived Value:** Pricing determines customer perception of product or service value. Higher pricing may denote superior quality, exclusivity, or luxury, whereas lower costs may indicate affordability or value for money.

- ❖ **Competitive Positioning:** Pricing strategy aligns a brand with competitors in the market. Companies can compete on price by offering lower costs than competitors, or they can differentiate themselves by charging more for perceived value or distinctive characteristics.

❖ **Revenue Generation:** Pricing immediately affects a company's revenue and profit. Effective pricing strategies maximize income by striking the right balance between pricing levels and sales volume.

❖ **Market Penetration:** Lowering prices can attract price-sensitive clients and help enter new markets or increase market share. This strategy could help you gain a footing in the market and raise brand awareness.

❖ **Brand Image:** Pricing influences brand image and perception. Premium price can boost a company's prestige and exclusivity, whereas bargain pricing may erode brand equity or sense of quality.

❖ **Product Positioning:** Pricing strategy should match product positioning in the market. A high-priced product may be positioned as a luxury or status symbol, whereas a low-priced product may appeal to budget-conscious customers.

- ❖ **Demand Management:** Dynamic pricing solutions, such surge pricing or price optimization algorithms, allow organizations to modify prices based on demand, supply, or market conditions. This helps to manage demand and increase revenue.

- ❖ **Customer Segmentation:** Pricing can be customized for specific customer segments based on their willingness to pay, purchasing habits, or demographics. This enables businesses to extract value from a variety of client categories and adapt pricing strategies accordingly.

- ❖ **Promotional Strategy:** Pricing is directly associated with promotional activities including discounts, promotions, and sales events. Strategic pricing promotions can boost short-term revenue, bring in new clients, and generate demand.

- ❖ **Adjusting to Changes in the Market:** Companies can adjust to shifts in the market, changes in competition, or changes in economic variables when they have pricing flexibility. Companies may stay competitive and react fast to changes in the market by implementing agile pricing strategies.

All things considered, pricing is a potent marketing tool that affects how customers act, how businesses are positioned in the market, how much money is made, and how people view their brand. To successfully drive growth and accomplish marketing goals, organizations must meticulously create pricing plans that are in line with company objectives and market conditions.

Section D: The Commodity Problem

Companies encounter what is known as the **"commodity problem"** when customers don't see much of a difference between their goods and services and those of their rivals. Because of this misconception, pricing wars break out, cutting into profit margins and making it harder to differentiate brands. A further in-depth analysis of the commodities dilemma and potential solutions follows:

Characteristics of the Commodity Problem:

- **Low Product Differentiation:** Products or services lack unique features or attributes that set them apart from competitors.

- **Price Sensitivity:** Customers largely focus their purchasing decisions on price, leading to price wars and downward pressure on profitability.

- **Erosion of Brand Value:** Inability to differentiate on grounds other than pricing can impair brand perception and loyalty.

- **Vulnerability to Market changes:** Businesses may struggle to maintain profitability in the face of market changes, shifting consumer preferences, or competition pressures.

Strategies to Address the Commodity Problem:

Value-added Differentiation:

- ❖ Identify opportunities to expand your product or service with additional features, advantages, or services that offer value for customers.
- ❖ Focus on addressing specific pain points or wants of your target market that competitors are not sufficiently addressing.

Brand Positioning:

- ❖ Develop a strong brand identity and positioning strategy that highlights distinctive value propositions, brand values, and customer experience.
- ❖ Communicate your brand story, mission, and values effectively to separate your brand from competition.

Customer Segmentation:

- ❖ Segment your target market based on unique demands, preferences, or demographics.
- ❖ Tailor your marketing messaging, pricing methods and product offerings to each segment to maximize relevance and appeal.

Innovation and R&D:

- ❖ Invest in research and development to continuously improve and innovate your products or services.
- ❖ Introduce new features, technology, or solutions that answer increasing client needs and differentiate your product from competition.

Customer Experience:

- ❖ Focus on offering great customer service and experience at every touchpoint.

❖ Invest in educating your team, optimizing processes, and introducing customer feedback methods to boost satisfaction and loyalty.

Distribution Methods:

❖ Explore alternative distribution methods or partnerships that enable access to new client segments or markets.

❖ Develop exclusive distribution agreements or alliances to reduce competition and boost brand visibility.

Content Marketing and Thought Leadership:

❖ Establish your brand as an expert in your sector using content marketing, thought leadership, and educational materials.

❖ Share relevant insights, expertise, and industry trends to position your business as a trustworthy advisor and differentiate from competition.

Price Optimization:

- ❖ Instead of engaging in price wars, focus on optimizing pricing strategies based on value perception, client segmentation, and market dynamics.

- ❖ Emphasize the value proposition and benefits of your solution to justify higher price where applicable.

Addressing the commodity problem, demands a holistic approach that goes beyond competing just on price. By concentrating on distinctiveness, value creation, and customer-centric strategies, firms can overcome the obstacles associated with commoditization and survive in competitive markets.

PART D: FINDING THE RIGHT MARKET - A STARVING CROWD

Section 1: Find The Right Market

Finding the correct market, frequently referred to as uncovering a **"starving crowd,"** entails recognizing a group of people with unmet requirements, interests, or issues that are not effectively handled by existing solutions. Here's a step-by-step way to finding the right market:

Uncover Pain Points and Needs:

- Conduct market research to uncover prevalent pain points, obstacles, or unmet needs among specific populations or industries.
- Look for problems or frustrations that consumers routinely encounter but have difficulty overcoming with existing solutions.

Explore Niche Markets:

- Consider niche markets or specialized segments within bigger businesses where there may be underserved or overlooked audiences.
- Look for groups of people with shared interests, passions, or special requirements that are not fully served by mainstream services.

Validate Demand:

- Test your assumptions and hypotheses by engaging with potential customers through surveys, interviews, or focus groups.
- Look for indications of great demand, high levels of participation, or readiness to pay for solutions to the highlighted problems or requirements.

Analyze Competition:

- Assess the competitive landscape to determine what solutions presently exist and how they satisfy the needs of the target market.
- Look for gaps or shortcomings in existing offerings that you may leverage on to give a superior option.

Define Your Unique Value Proposition:

- Determine how your product or service can differentiate itself from competitors and provide compelling value to the target market.
- Identify your unique selling points, features, or benefits that address the specific needs or desires of the starving crowd.

Test and Iterate:

- Start small by testing your product or service with a subset of the target market to gain feedback and refine your offering.

+ Iterate based on customer insights, market input, and performance indicators to consistently improve and adjust your approach.

Build Ties:

+ Cultivate ties with potential customers, influencers, and stakeholders within the target market.

+ Engage in communities, forums, or social media groups where your audience congregates to obtain insights, establish reputation, and develop trust.

Grow Responsibly:

+ Once you've proven demand and fine-tuned your offering, grow your marketing efforts to reach a bigger audience.

+ Focus on sustainable growth techniques that allow you to retain quality, customer satisfaction, and profitability as you expand.

Stay Agile and Adaptive:

- Remain open to feedback and market developments, and be prepared to pivot or adapt your approach as needed.
- Continuously monitor market developments, client preferences, and competition dynamics to stay ahead of the curve.

By following these steps, you may effectively discover and capitalize on opportunities to serve a starving public with solutions that suit their needs and desires, thereby setting your firm for success in the marketplace.

Section 2: Changing The Perceived Value Or Worth Of A Product Or Service

Enhance Features or Quality:

- Improve the features, functionality, or quality of your product or service to raise its perceived value.

- Add new features or enhancements that satisfy client wants or preferences, making the offering more attractive and valuable.

Highlight Benefits and Value Proposition:

- Clearly explain the benefits and value proposition of your product or service to customers.
- Emphasize how your offering addresses specific problems, fulfills desires, or enhances the consumer experience, so raising its perceived value.

Improve Packaging and Presentation:

- Enhance the packaging, branding, and presentation of your product or service to generate a more premium or desired perception.
- Invest in expert design, branding, and packaging that correspond with your target market's preferences and expectations.

Offer Additional Services or Bonuses:

+ Include additional services, bonuses, or add-ons to boost the perceived value of your business.

+ Provide complementary services, longer warranties, or bonus features that boost the total value proposition for clients.

Adjust Pricing plan:

+ Strategically adjust your pricing plan to reflect the perceived worth of your product or service.

+ Consider boosting costs if your providing gives excellent quality, features, or benefits compared to competitors. • Alternatively, offer discounts or promotions to make your offering more accessible or attractive to price-sensitive clients.

Leverage Social Proof and Testimonials:

+ Showcase favorable reviews, testimonials, or endorsements from delighted consumers to boost the perceived worth of your business.

+ Highlight real-life examples or case studies that highlight the tangible benefits and consequences customers have experienced with your product or service.

Create Exclusivity or Scarcity:

+ Introduce characteristics of exclusivity or scarcity to improve the perceived value of your item.

+ Limit availability, offer limited-edition versions, or create exclusive membership programs to make your product or service more desirable and valuable.

Provide Exceptional Customer Service:

+ Deliver exceptional customer service and assistance to enhance the entire experience and perception of your brand.

+ Invest in training your people, developing efficient processes, and focusing customer satisfaction to underline the value of your service.

Continuously Innovate and Adapt:

- Stay ahead of the competition by continuously developing and adjusting your product or service to satisfy changing client wants and preferences.
- Monitor market trends, receive feedback, and iterate on your offering to keep its relevance and perceived value over time.

By employing these tactics, you may effectively improve or enhance the perceived value of your product or service, making it more desirable and valuable to your target audience.

Section 3: Why The Majority Of Marketing Is A Scam

For organizations, marketing can occasionally feel like a money pit when it doesn't produce the expected outcomes or return on investment (ROI). There are various things that may influence this view.

- ❖ **Lack of a Clear plan:** Resources may be allocated inefficiently, resulting in wasted spending and little effect on results, in the absence of a well-defined marketing plan that is in line with business goals.

- ❖ **Ineffective Targeting:** Marketing campaigns with inadequate targeting may miss their target audience or fail to connect with prospects who are most likely to become customers. Lower ROI and resource waste result from this.

- ❖ **Overemphasis on Tactics:** Dispersed efforts and diminished impact might result from concentrating just on tactics or channels in the absence of a clear plan. Spending money haphazardly on several marketing initiatives without a well-defined plan can squander resources without producing noticeable outcomes.

- ❖ **Failure to Measure and Analyze:** It might be difficult to evaluate the success of campaigns and come to wise judgments when marketing metrics are not tracked and analyzed properly. Without accurate measurement, companies might keep funding unsuccessful tactics without understanding it.

❖ **Short-term Focus:** An obsession with immediate outcomes could cause one to put short-term strategies ahead of long-term brand development initiatives. While quick wins are important, ignoring long-term plans might impede profitable and sustained growth.

❖ **Inadequate Testing and Optimization:** Businesses are unable to recognize and take advantage of chances for improvement when marketing initiatives are not adequately tested and optimized. Marketing initiatives risk stagnating without iteration and improvement, which would mean squandered money and lower returns.

❖ **Lack of Differentiation:** Marketing turns into a race to the bottom based on features or pricing when companies are unable to set themselves apart from rivals. The perceived money pit that results from this commoditization is caused by a decrease in the effectiveness of marketing campaigns.

- **Misallocation of Resources:** Inefficient expenditure and less-than-ideal outcomes can emerge from poor resource allocation, which includes investing excessively in unproductive channels or ignoring new opportunities.

- **Ignoring the Customer Experience:** When marketing efforts aren't met or the customer experience is neglected, trust and loyalty are damaged, which leads to lost revenue when customers leave or stop being involved.

- **External Factors:** Unexpected market upheavals, behavioral changes in consumers, or economic downturns can affect the efficacy of marketing initiatives, making it difficult to get targeted outcomes even with large investments.

Businesses should prioritize long-term brand-building efforts, have a clear plan, target the correct demographic, measure performance, test, and optimize campaigns to prevent marketing from turning into a money pit. Businesses can increase the efficacy and return on investment (ROI) of their marketing initiatives by strategically allocating resources and iteratively improving strategies in light of data and insights.

Section 4: The Secret to Making Your Audience Notice, Hear, and Understand You

Having good communication and engagement methods is essential to being understood, heard, and seen. Here are some essential ideas to help you do this:

Clarity and Simplicity:

- ✓ Make sure your audience can understand your message by communicating it succinctly and clearly.

✓ To ensure that everyone can understand your message, use plain language, stay away from jargon, and cut out any superfluous detail.

The Audience-Centric Approach:

✓ Recognize the requirements, preferences, and problems of your audience in order to craft a message that will appeal to them.

✓ Show empathy and comprehension for your audience by using language and pictures that they can identify with.

Active Listening:

✓ Use active listening techniques to fully comprehend the issues, criticisms, and points of view of your audience.

✓ Promote candid communication, pose inquiries, and genuinely listen to others.

Transparency and Authenticity:

- ✓ Show your personality, values, and beliefs in your communication by being sincere and real.
- ✓ Establish credibility by being open and honest about your goals, course of action, and any obstacles or restrictions your audience might encounter.

Captivating Storytelling:

- ✓ Employ storytelling strategies to draw listeners in, arouse feelings, and deliver your point in an unforgettable manner.
- ✓ Create stories that speak to the experiences, goals, and values of your audience to increase the relatability and effectiveness of your message.

Visual and Multisensory Communication:

- ✓ Use visual aids to support your message and improve comprehension, such as pictures, films, or infographics.

✓ Use multimedia content that appeals to a variety of senses to make communication more immersive and interesting.

Consistency and Repetition:

✓ Use a variety of communication channels and touchpoints to consistently reinforce important themes.

✓ Over time, repetition increases the likelihood that your message will be seen, heard, and understood by strengthening memory and comprehension.

Feedback and Iteration:

✓ Ask for feedback from your audience to find out how well they comprehend and interpret your message.

✓ Make adjustments to your communication strategy based on feedback, clearing up any miscommunications or areas of confusion.

Inclusivity and Accessibility:

- ✓ Make sure your message is understandable to everyone in your audience, including people from different backgrounds or with disabilities.
- ✓ Offer substitute formats, including subtitles, transcripts, or translations, to suit varying requirements and inclinations.

Empowerment and Action:

- ✓ Encourage your audience to take concrete action by giving them explicit calls to action.
- ✓ Promote involvement, teamwork, and participation to foster a sense of responsibility and connection with your message.

You may improve the effectiveness of your communication and raise the possibility that your audience will see, hear, and understand you by putting these ideas into practice.

Section 5: The Secret Weapon That Will Grow Your Business

The "secret weapon" that can develop your firm rapidly is a conglomeration of success-oriented tactics, techniques, and mindsets. Although there isn't a single magic solution, the following crucial components might act as potent growth accelerators:

Customer-Centric Approach:

- Put your customers' needs first and try your best to understand and meet their demands.
- Develop trusting relationships, pay attention to criticism, and never stop trying to go above and beyond for customers.

Innovation and Adaptability:

- To set your goods, services, or company model apart, embrace innovation and creativity.

- Remain flexible and responsive to changing consumer tastes, technology breakthroughs, and industry trends.

Strategic Marketing:

- Create an all-encompassing marketing plan that successfully reaches your intended clientele.
- Reach and interact with your audience using a combination of online and offline channels, and track the return on investment of your marketing initiatives.

High-quality goods or services:

- Gain your clients' trust and loyalty by providing them with goods and services of the highest caliber.
- To stay ahead of the competition and be relevant in the market, concentrate on innovation and constant development.

Powerful Branding and Differentiation:

- Create a distinctive brand identity that connects with your target market and makes you stand out from rivals.
- Express your unique value proposition in a clear and concise manner, and fulfill your brand promise every time.

Strategic Alliances and Partnerships:

- Increase your capabilities and reach by working with companies that complement yours or with industry partners.
- Look for partnerships that will benefit both parties and allow you to expand into new areas, acquire resources, or improve your services.

Operational Excellence:

- Optimize productivity and efficiency by streamlining your internal operations and processes.

- Make investments in automation, technology, and staff development to maximize productivity and provide reliable outcomes.

Customer Experience Focus:

- Give top priority to providing outstanding customer experiences at each point of contact.
- Make investments in systems, technologies, and training that will help you deliver experiences that are memorable, smooth, and customized.

Data-Driven Decision-Making:

- Make strategic decisions and promote ongoing development using data and analytics.
- Track consumer behavior, keep an eye on key performance indicators (KPIs), and use insights to find opportunities and reduce risks.

Resilience and Persistence:

- Develop a resilient and persistent mindset to get over obstacles and failures.
- Remain dedicated to your vision and objectives, and show yourself open to changing course, pivoting, and enduring hardship.

Section 6: The straightforward SB7 Framework

While there isn't a one "secret weapon" for company growth, incorporating these essential components into your business plan will greatly increase your chances of success and long-term, sustainable growth.

Below is a summary of every element:

1. Strategy:

- ✓ Create a precise and targeted plan that describes your company's objectives, target market, competitive landscape, and value offer.
- ✓ Outline your goals, both short- and long-term, and create a plan of action to reach them.

2. Sales:

- ✓ Put into practice efficient sales techniques and procedures to boost sales and expand the company.
- ✓ Determine who your target clientele is, learn about their wants, and adjust your sales strategy to suit them.
- ✓ To turn prospects into clients, use sales strategies like lead generation, prospecting, and closing.

3. Service:

- ✓ To increase client satisfaction and loyalty, offer outstanding customer service and support.

✓ Concentrate on providing top-notch goods and services that either match or surpass client expectations.

✓ Establish trusting connections with clients, pay attention to their opinions, and work tirelessly to make their experience better every time.

4. Systems:

✓ To assure consistency, improve productivity, and streamline operations, establish effective systems and processes.

✓ Use automation technologies and technological solutions to streamline operations, cut down on labor-intensive tasks, and maximize resource use.

✓ Consistently assess and enhance your systems to adjust to evolving business requirements and enhance overall effectiveness.

5. Staff:

- ✓ Assemble a bright, driven group of people who share your values and company objectives.
- ✓ Make investments in attracting, educating, and keeping exceptional personnel, and offer chances for career advancement and progress.
- ✓ Encourage a culture of cooperation, creativity, and ongoing learning in the workplace.

6. Scale:

- ✓ Create plans for growing your company's operations and branching out into other markets or industry sectors.
- ✓ Determine prospects for expansion, such introducing novel goods or services, venturing into uncharted territories, or focusing on fresh customer segments.

- ✓ Methodically plan and carry out expansion projects, considering resource distribution, risk mitigation, and tactical alliances.

7. Success:

- ✓ Define what success means to your company and set up metrics to monitor development and output.
- ✓ Track key performance indicators (KPIs) for important areas such as sales, profitability, and customer happiness.
- ✓ To promote continuous development and success, assess your performance often, acknowledge your successes, and absorb lessons from your mistakes.

These seven critical areas—Strategy, Sales, Service, Systems, Staff, Scale, and Success—help organizations build a solid basis for expansion and purposefully and clearly traverse the challenges of entrepreneurship.

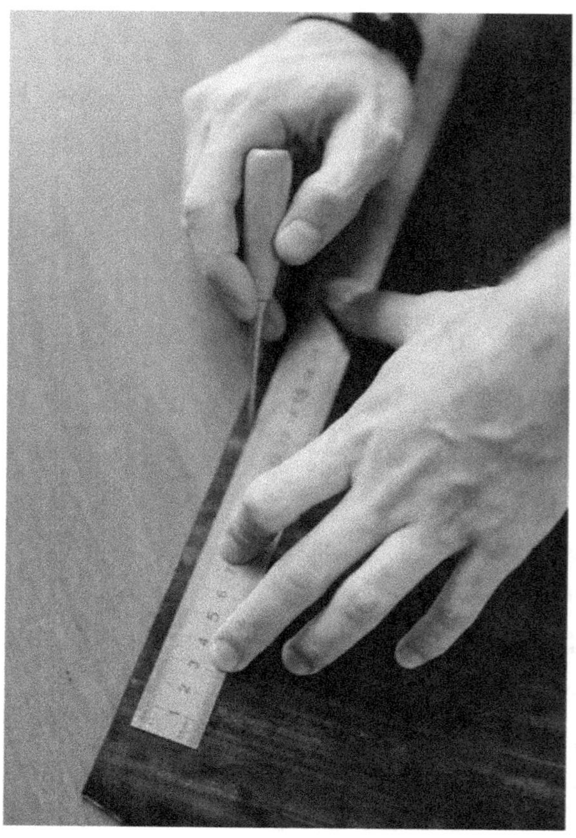

AUDIENCE

PART E: THE EXPERT SECRETS

Section 1: Summary of Expert Secrets

Expert Secrets is all about mastering the art of converting web visitors into lifelong clients, which you will achieve by becoming an expert. This means that you will become a movement leader rather than just someone who sells services or products.

To accomplish this, Russell delves deeply into four frameworks: establishing your movement, establishing belief, "10x secrets" one-to-many selling, become your ideal customer's guide

Section 2: Creating Your Movement

To start a movement, you need three things:

- ❖ An expert or guide.
- ❖ A new chance to provide to your audience.

❖ A future-oriented cause to unite the tribe

1. Become An Expert

Russell outlines his five-phase methodology for becoming your tribe's lead.

Phase 1: The Dreamer

Leadership and how to become an expert are skills that you can learn.

Experiment with everything, discover something that piques your attention, and immerse yourself in it until you master it.

Phase #2: Assuming The Identity Of The Reporter

Your own knowledge isn't sufficient. You should interview other specialists to get various perspectives.

Phase 3: Create Your Own Frameworks.

At some point, we recognize that the only way to continue growing is to change our focus away from personal development and toward giving.

Phase 4: Work For Free While Serving Your Eventual Dream Customer.

Test your framework on yourself and others to check it generates the same (or better) outcomes.

Phase 5: Becoming An Expert.

Once you've completed the first four steps, you'll be able to lead others as an expert.

2. New Opportunity (Your Offer)

Every product is promoted based on three basic markets or desires: health, wealth, and relationships.

When the three major markets grew too competitive, firms began to create submarkets.

For example, there are hundreds of strategies to achieve internal health goals, such as weight loss, nutrition, strength training, and so on.

People formed "niches" after the submarkets became competitive, a specific approach to meet the submarket's want, which in turn fulfills the fundamental desire.

For example:

✓ Core market: Health

✓ Submarket: Nutrition

✓ Niche: ketogenic diets, cancer diets, etc.

Rather than attempting to improve on someone else's product or service, establish your own unique opportunity (your own niche) to differentiate yourself from the competition.

3- The Future-Based Cause (Your Movement)

Proverbs 29:18 states, "Where there is no vision, people perish."

Your role as an expert is to lead your ideal clients on a journey of achievement and transformation.

To achieve your goals, consider:

- Creating a "platform" to lead your ideal customers
- Giving them a new identity
- Offering milestone awards to motivate them
- Partnering with a social mission.

Creating Belief

In this segment, Russell delves further into the "Story" component of the "Hook, Story, Offer" framework he introduced in Dotcom Secrets.

Your stories are important to your sales because they frame your offer and boost its perceived worth.

One crucial concept is "the epiphany bridge": a story that takes people through the emotional experience that sparked your enthusiasm for the new possibility you're providing.

How to Build It: A Five-Step Framework

Phase 1: The Backstory.

1. What is your backstory that gives you a vested stake in your journey?
2. What is the DESIRE or outcome you wish to achieve? Desires can be both external and inward.
3. What OLD VEHICLES have you used in the past to achieve the same result that did not work for you?

Phase #2: The Journey

1. What was THE CALL or the reason you embarked on this journey?
2. Who or what is THE VILLAIN preventing you from achieving success?
3. What happens if you don't succeed on your journey?

Phase 3: New Opportunity.

1. Who was the GUIDE who gave you your epiphany?

2. What was the EPIPHANY that you experienced?

3. What new opportunity have you generated as a result of this epiphany?

Phase #4: The Framework

1. What is the STRATEGY of frameworks you built to help you attain your goals?

2. What results did you achieve by following the frameworks?

3. What were THE OTHERS' RESULTS from using your framework?

Phase 5: Achievement And Transformation.

1. What was the end result that you achieved? (External wants).

2. How did you grow during this journey? (Internal wants)

If you have 10 or 20 minutes, answer all of the questions, but just use the headlines if you want to tell the same narrative in 30 seconds.

It is also vital to note key components of effective storytelling, such as simplicity, "kinda like" bring (connecting complicated concepts to what clients already know), and making them feel.

"10X Secrets": One-To-Many Selling

When you sell face-to-face, you can ask specific questions, receive personalized feedback, and resolve objections right away. You can't have that in a funnel, so make sure your presentation addresses all of the arguments that will arise for as many individuals as possible.

Russell approaches the problem as follows: The ideal webinar framework. It features three stages:

1. The biggest domino

2. The three secrets.

3. Stack and close

The Large Domino

Every product has one Big Domino, one thing that, if knocked down, removes all minor objections and opposition.

If you can persuade your prospect of the One Thing (the Big Domino) that will overcome their reservations, they will buy.

The Three Secrets

If the Big Domino does not fall on the first try, you will need to challenge your audience's other incorrect ideas. These are:

The vehicle: any additional misconceptions they may have about your new offer. Internal beliefs: misguided views about their own ability to capitalize on the new chance. External beliefs are incorrect assumptions about outside causes that may prevent them from succeeding.

The Stack And Close

When selling, the last thing you show prospects is what they remember.

As a result, when you add pieces to your offer one at a time on the same slide, your prospect can see the value grow right in front of their eyes.

Become Your Ideal Customer's Guide.

Your role as an expert is to help your ideal consumers through their own Hero's Two Journeys (the journeys of achievement and transformation). How to do that?

Backstory: Identify the red oceans where your prospects are frustrated and stuck, and begin throwing out hooks to capture their attention.

adventure: invite them to abandon their daily lives and join you on an adventure.

New opportunity: provide the new opportunity.

It's also critical to practice your presentation ahead of time. Most people make the mistake of creating a presentation they believe is good, recording it once, and then putting it in their funnels.

If you do this, you'll have no idea what people's true objections are.

SOCIAL
ENGAGEMENT

PLANNING

CONCLUSION

I met Olivia on a Tuesday morning, when she explained the challenges she was facing as an entrepreneur, battling to earn enough to pay the bills. She barely makes $1,000 every week. I gave her one of my numerous books title **"The One-Week Marketing Plan"**; she chose to check it out.

The primary day of planning her business' promoting plan centered on tracking down her specialty. Olivia understood that her specialization in the public speaking preparing could help her stand apart from the opposition and draw in additional clients She used the One Week Marketing Plan's strategies, such as creating buyer personas, engaging her audience through email marketing, optimizing her Google My Business listing, and creating social media channels, over the following few days.

Olivia's business began to flourish as a direct result of her efforts. She started drawing in new clients and supporting her deals, in the end arriving where she was making $10,000 every week. The Multi Week Promoting Plan had assisted her with changing her business, and she was thankful for the functional aide that had given her simple to-carry out procedures to draw in new clients and lift deals

Olivia's example of overcoming adversity fills in as a motivation for other entrepreneurs who are battling to earn a living wage. By following the Multi Week Promoting Plan and zeroing in on finding their specialty, they also can develop their organizations and increment their income.

To sum up, the one-week marketing plan has shown to be a game-changing resource for a great number of people who are trying to succeed in business. It has enabled entrepreneurs to achieve amazing growth and observable outcomes in a short amount of time with its strategic approach and concrete tactics.

Businesses have been able to extend their customer base seize new possibilities, and generate more money by carefully adhering to the plan's guiding principles. Every facet of the one-week marketing plan, from locating niche markets to utilizing digital marketing platforms, has helped numerous people achieve success.

As we consider this plan's effects, it becomes clear that its efficacy comes from both its simplicity and its capacity to produce quantifiable results. We've seen time and time again that committing even one week to targeted marketing initiatives can result in massive returns and advance companies toward their objectives.

YOUR ONLINE MARKETING STRATEGY FOR THE WEEK

1	MONDAY	MASTERING STORYTELLING	
	Morning	**Afternoon**	**Evening**
	Craft Your Brand Story	Develop Compelling Content	Social Media Engagement
	Define your brand's narrative, values, and mission.	Create engaging content that aligns with your brand story.	Share your brand story on social media platforms.
	Identify key storytelling elements that resonate with your audience.	Utilize various mediums (text, images, videos) to tell your brand story effectively.	Engage with your audience by responding to comments and fostering conversations.
2	Tuesday	Crafting Irresistible Offers	
	Morning	**Afternoon**	**Evening**
	Understand Your Audience	Create Irresistible Offers	Launch and Promote
	Analyze your	Develop	Launch your

	target audience's needs, desires, and pain points.	compelling offers that stand out in the market.	irresistible offers across relevant channels.
	Tailor your product or service offerings to address their specific requirements.	Ensure your offers provide significant value and solve your audience's problems.	Develop a promotional strategy to generate initial interest and excitement.
3	**Wednesday**	**Implementing Expert Secrets**	
	Morning	**Afternoon**	**Evening**
	Learn from Experts	Implement Expert Strategies	Analyze Results
	Consume content from industry experts and successful entrepreneurs.	Apply expert tactics to your marketing plan.	Review the performance of your marketing efforts.
	Identify key strategies and secrets that align with your goals.	Optimize your campaigns based on the insights gained from	Identify what worked well and areas for improvement.

		industry experts.	
4	**Thursday**	**Marketing Tracker Review**	
	Morning	**Afternoon**	**Evening**
	Track Key Metrics	Analyze Data	Adjust Marketing Plan
	. Use the Marketing Tracker to monitor KPIs.	Dive deeper into data analytics.	Make adjustments to your marketing plan based on the insights gained.
	Assess progress toward your revenue goal	Identify trends and patterns that can inform your next steps.	Set goals for the next phase of your campaign.
5	**Friday**	**Continued Optimization**	
	Morning	**Afternoon**	**Evening**
	Optimization Strategies	Content Refresh	Community Engagement
	Implement optimization strategies based on your analysis.	Update and refresh your content to keep it relevant.	Engage with your audience in the online community.
	A/B test different elements to refine your	Leverage user-generated content or	Address questions, provide support, and foster a sense of community around

	method.	reviews.	your brand.
6	**Saturday**	**Reflection and Planning**	
	Morning	**Afternoon**	**Evening**
	Review the Week	Goal Setting	Relax and Recharge
	Reflect on the week's activities and achievements.	Set new goals for the upcoming week.	Take time to relax and recharge for the next week.
	Celebrate successes and learn from challenges.	Align goals with insights gained from the previous week's performance.	Prepare mentally for new challenges and opportunities.

PRAISE FOR RIGHT ACROSS THE BAY

"RIGHT ACROSS THE BAY is an enthralling thriller with more than its fair share of twists and turns. Quinn Avery displays a knack for hooking in her readers right from the opening paragraph, blending moments of ripe romantic intrigue with high-tension thrills."
-IndieReader.com

"A small town murder mystery that is anything but small. Right Across the Bay is a must-read whodunnit infused with romance, betrayal and an unforgettable finale."
-BestThrillers.com

"Without a doubt one of the best thrillers I have ever read, I devoured this in one sitting literally unable to put it down. An incredible gripping, unpredictable read full of secrets and twists. An absolute must read."
-ericas_bookreviews

"I absolutely loved this book, it was a really quick and easy read. I found it engaging, fast paced and hooked me straight in"
-joebella_p_reads

"This one took me by surprise more than once. I was not expecting the culprit at all and had a couple of jaw-dropping moments as I read."
-2manybooks2littletime

PRAISE FOR LOST GIRLS OF KATO

ARMOR BOOK AWARDS SEMI-FINALIST

*"A clever psychic thriller steeped in 80s nostalgia
that will delight Stranger Things fans and
anyone looking for a great read."*
-BestThrillers.com

*"This is exactly what I would describe my favorite
genre to be - but with a little unique twist that
I absolutely didn't see coming!"*
- book_a_holic_17

*"I couldn't put this book down. It had the easy reading
flow of a Nicholas Sparks book with a mystery
murder who done it feel."*
-Goodreads

*"I read the entire thing in one night, staying up way too late!
Best book I've read in ages. The way the story progresses is
absolute perfection."*
-Instagram

*"The way Quinn Avery brought the two decades together, the
suspense, the intrigue was amazing. I had no idea how it
would end until everything was divulged in the end."*
-Goodreads